TIM JEFFS ART
Animal Sketches
Wild Cats

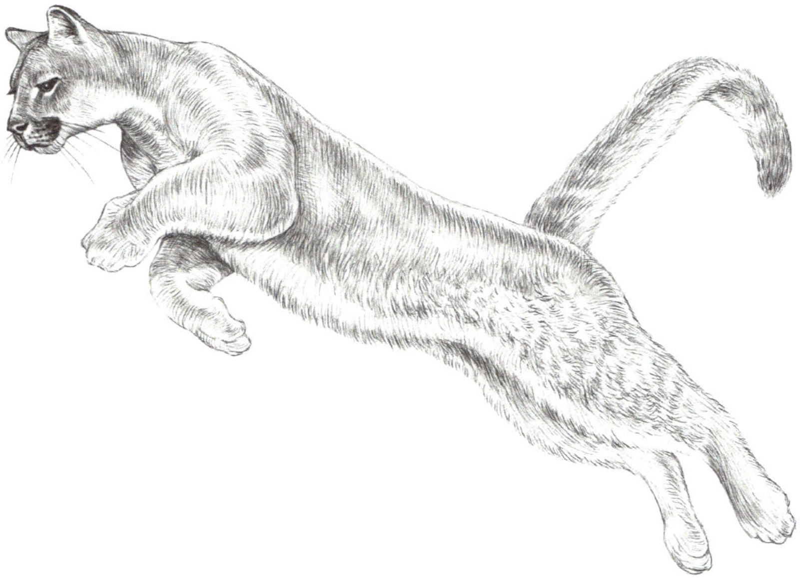

A Special Edition Coloring Book

For Jane, Jenna and Harrison

Dedicated to all of the wonderful colorists who have supported my art and made my drawings more beautiful with their colors, and all the precious creatures that we live among.
A special thank you to Jo Warren for her continued support, beautiful colorings and the coloring lesson that make this book so much more special!

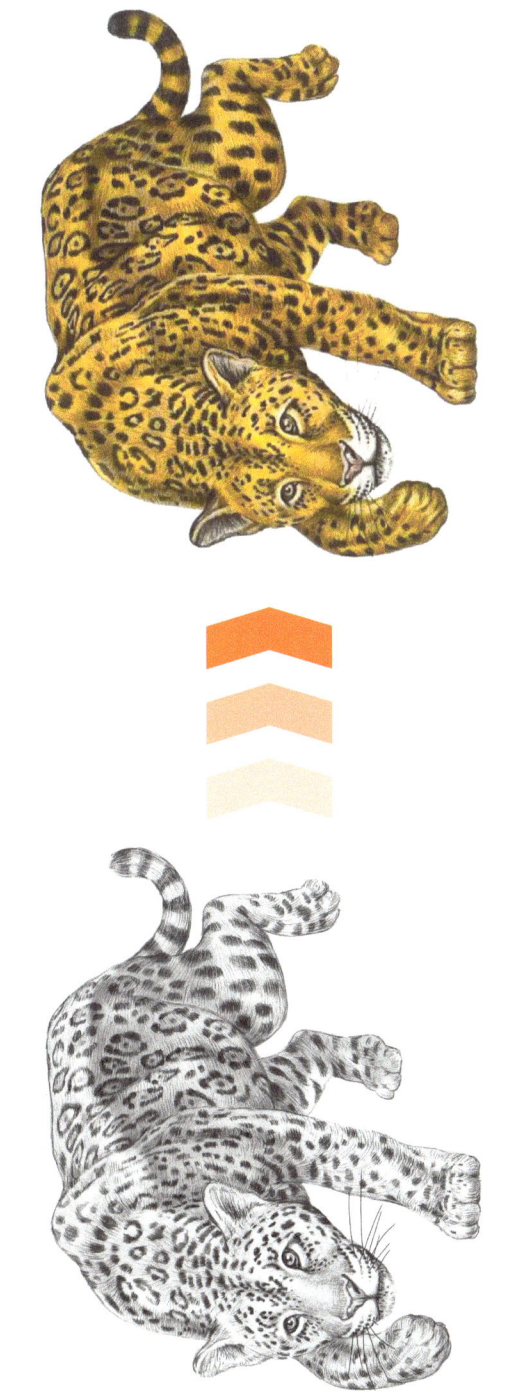

© Copyright 2021 Tim Jeffs Art

All rights reserved. No part of this publication may be reproduced or distributed in any form without the prior written permission of Tim Jeffs Art.

Tim Jeffs Art

376 East Madison Avenue, Dumont, NJ 07628

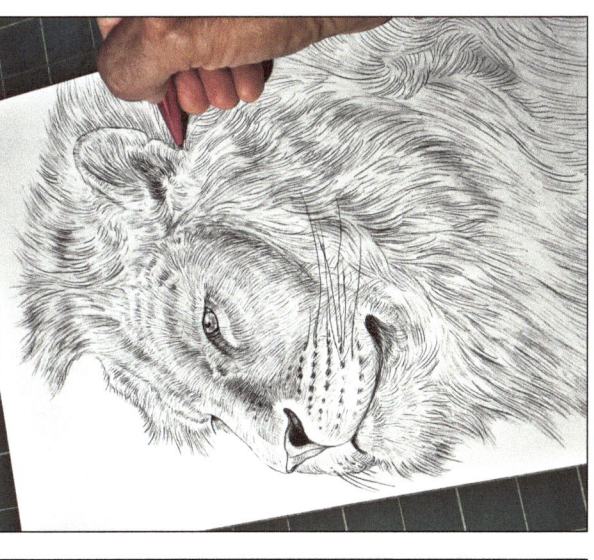

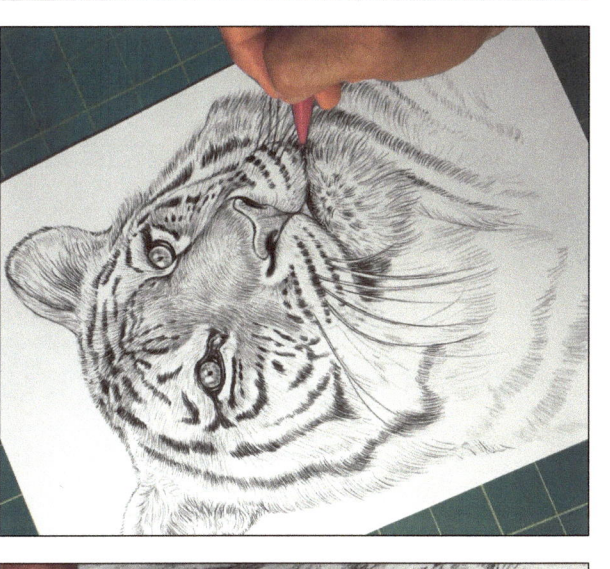

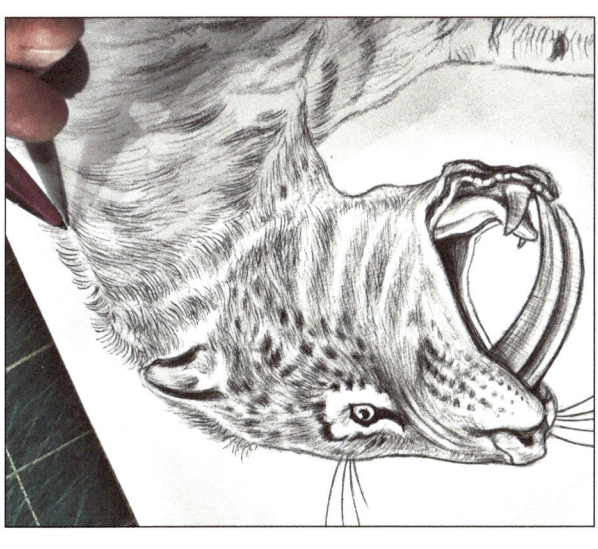

Wild Cats Sketchbook Thoughts

I have always been attracted to the detailed and diverse patterns that adorn wild cats. These fascinating creatures are wonderful subjects to draw. Cats exhibit the most diverse fur patterns of all terrestrial carnivores. Their spots, stripes and shading are exciting to draw in black and white, and even better for colorists to add their creative colors too.

In this coloring book I chose a variety of wild cats. It was hard choosing just 15 cats out of the nearly 40 species of wild cats in the world. I decided to choose a variety of cats including large and small, cats with a thriving conservation status and those who are struggling to survive. Also, I couldn't resist including the ultimate of all cats, the Saber-tooth tiger or Smilodon, who has been extinct for 10's of thousands of years.

I hope you enjoy coloring this group of wild cat sketches as much as I enjoyed drawing them, and I know that with your colors, you will bring them roaring to life! Have fun!

GRAYSCALE COLORING LESSON
Cheetah

Lesson level: Easy

Coloring the *Cheetah*

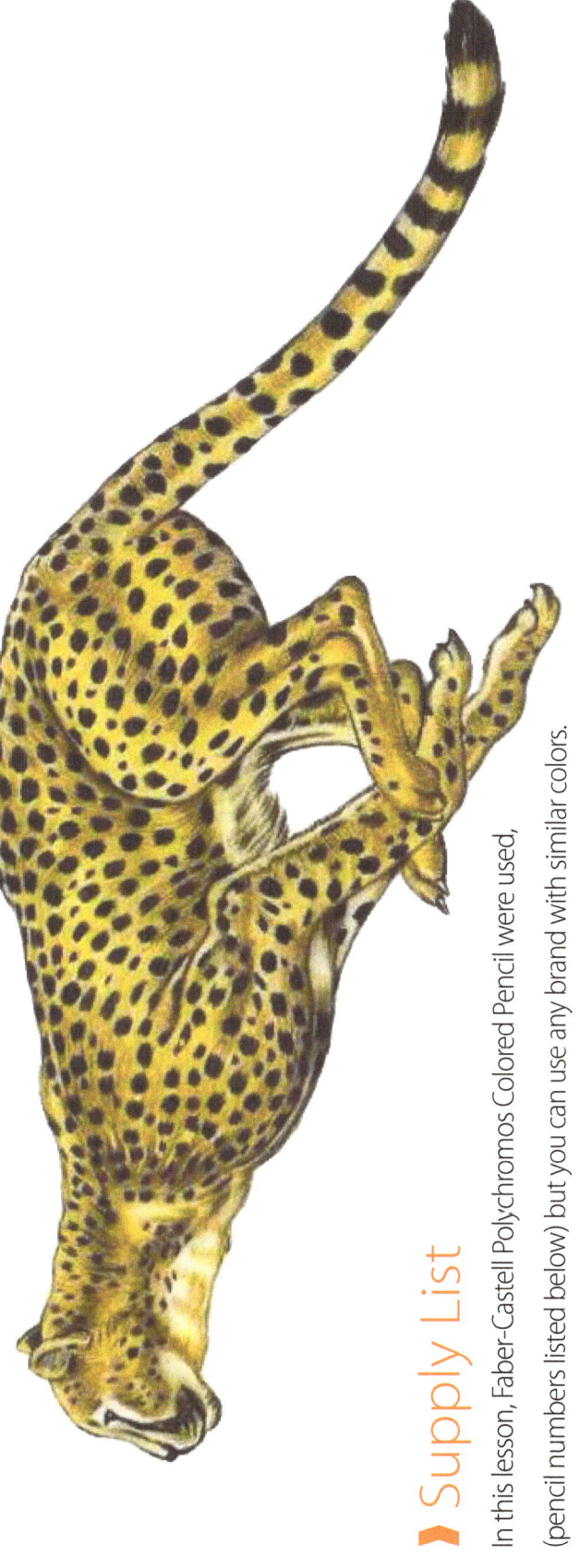

On the next page I will walk you through the coloring of the cheetah which is on page 2 of this coloring book. Cheetahs are the fastest land animal reaching speeds up to 128 km/h or 80mph. For this drawing I wanted to capture the glory of the cheetah in full sprint. As you color it I hope you can imagine the cheetah speeding by you! This beautiful coloring of the cheetah was done by Jo Warren. Many thanks for her creative and inspirational step-by-step photos.

▶ Supply List

In this lesson, Faber-Castell Polychromos Colored Pencil were used, (pencil numbers listed below) but you can use any brand with similar colors.

1) **The coloring page can be found on page 2**
2) **Colors:** Raw Umber #180, Burnt Ochre #187, Dark Cadmium Yellow #108, Light Yellow Ochre #183, Bistre #179, Black #199
3) **Pencil Sharpener:** An electric pencils sharpener is easy to use and works best to keep your pencils extra sharp and your hand less sore. But if you don't have one, no problem. A hand pencil sharpener works just fine too.

GRAYSCALE COLORING LESSON

Cheetah

Cheetah

Supplies needed: 6 colored pencils

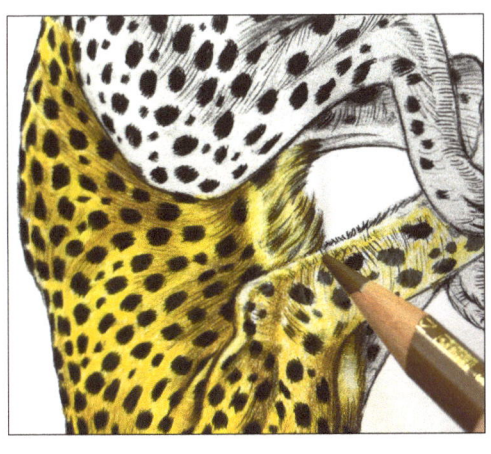

Step 1. Start by coloring a base layer of (#183) Light Yellow Orchre and then add (#180) Raw Umber to darken the forehead and cheeks.

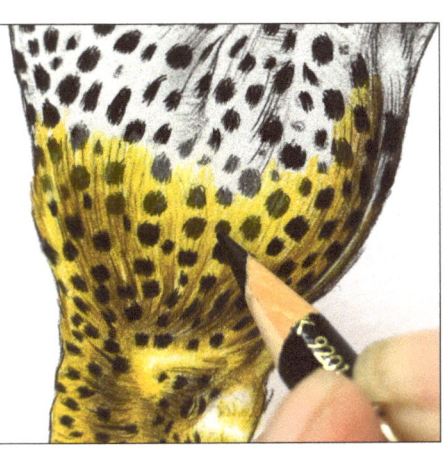

Step 2. Around the eye, mouth, neck and shoulder leave the paper uncolored to create white without having to color white.

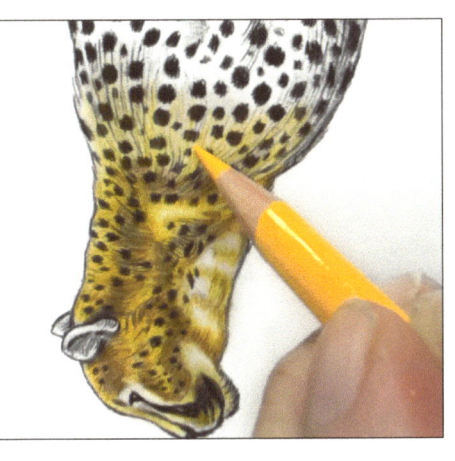

Step 3. To create depth and shape to your cheetah after coloring your base layer with (#183) darken the outer edges of the shoulder, chest and back with (#180) and finally using (#179) Bistre color strokes following the fur lines in the drawing.

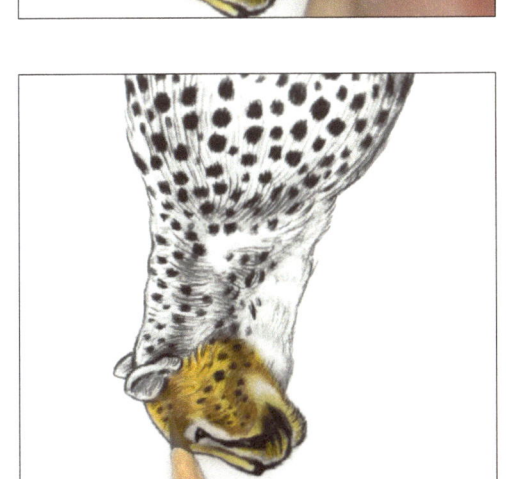

Step 4. Using (#187) Burnt Ochre color along the back edge of the cheetah's front leg slightly in from the edge with short stokes. This will add movement to the cheetah's fur as if it's flowing in the wind.

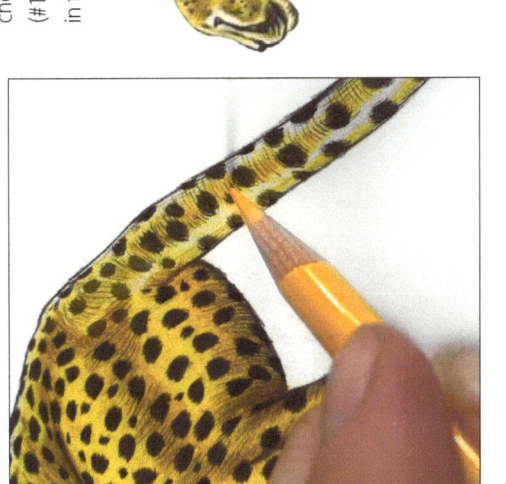

Step 5. Darken the cheetah's spots using (#199) Black to give them definition. This will make the cheetah's spots pop!

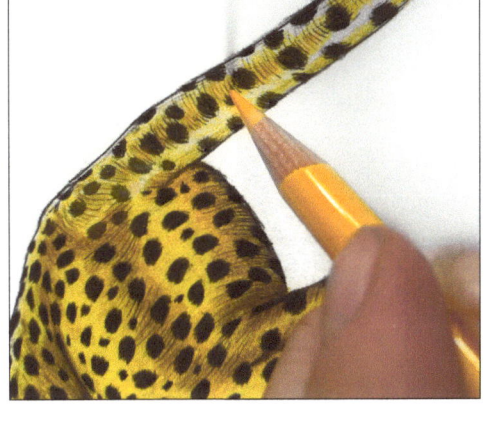

Step 6. Finaly add accents of color using (#108) Dark Cadmium Yellow on the underside of the back leg and the center of the tail.

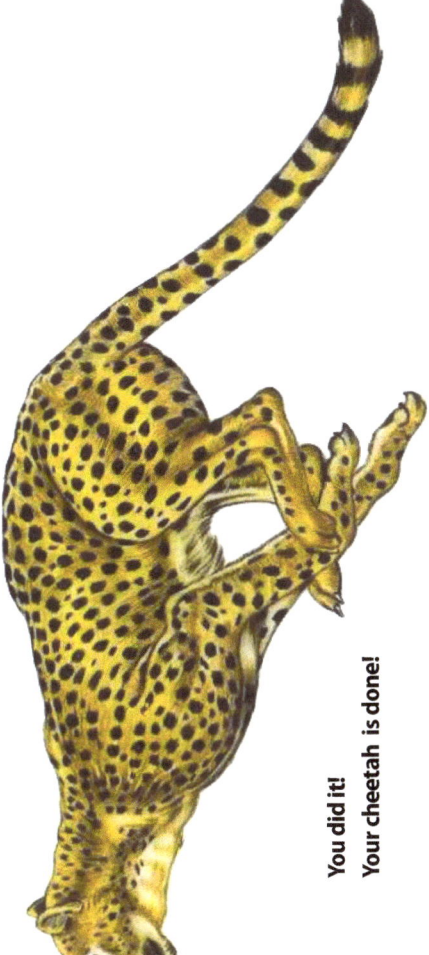

You did it!
Your cheetah is done!

Coloring Steps by Jo Warren

Spreading Awareness through *Coloring*

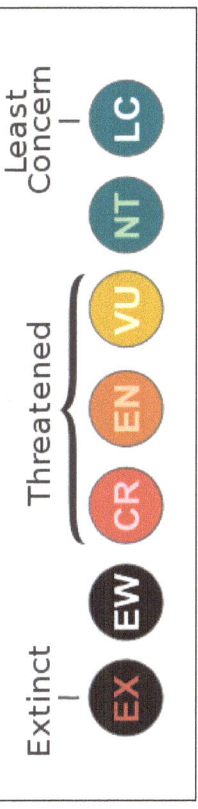

The list consists of 7 categories. From Least Concerned all the way to Extinct. Here are the definitions of each category:

- **LEAST CONCERN (LC):** A species that has been evaluated but not qualified for any other category on the list.
- **NEAR THREATENED (NT):** A species that may be considered threatened with extinction in the near future.
- **VULNERABLE (VU):** A species likely to become endangered unless the circumstances that are threatening its survival and reproduction improve.
- **ENDANGERED (EN):** A species that is considered very likely to become extinct.
- **CRITICALLY ENDANGERED (CR):** A species that is facing an extremely high risk of becoming extinct in the wild.
- **EXTINCT IN THE WILD (EW):** A species that is only known by living members kept in captivity or as a naturalized population outside its historic range due to massive habitat loss.
- **EXTINCT (EX):** A species that has been terminated.

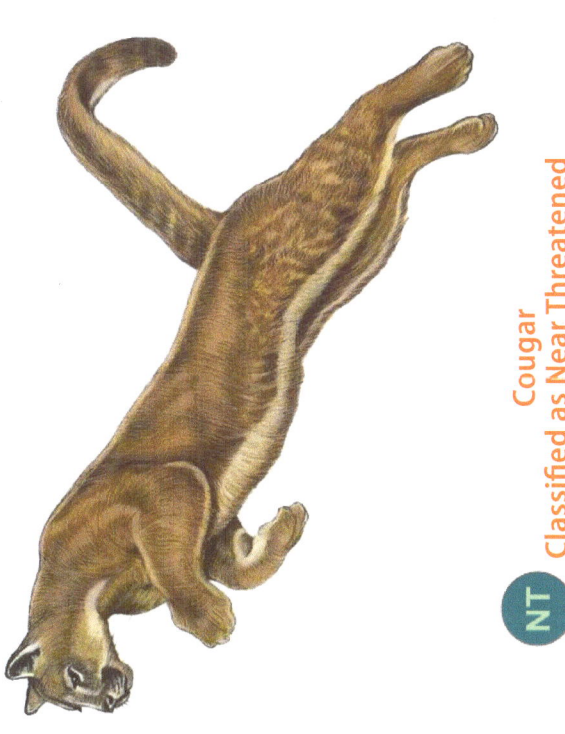

NT Cougar
Classified as Near Threatened

I truly believe that raising awareness through the sharing of my artwork is a fantastic way to educate people about conservation. And coloring animals is a beautiful way to learn about them as you enjoy a relaxing and fun pastime. On the following page, I listed the wild cats statuses on the *International Union for Conservation of Nature's (IUCN)* conservation list. I think it's important to include the *(IUCN)* conservation list so people understand the classifications more clearly. To the right is an overview of the IUCN's conservation list, which breaks animals' conservation statuses into several categories. Knowing what these categories mean and the animals that are included in them is extremely important. **Together through art we can change the world!**

Tim Jeffs
Animal Artist

Learn about the Wild Cats

Before you start coloring, it's important to learn where the wild cats in this book live or lived and know their conservation status. Many of them are doing well and thriving and are considered least concern; a few are vulnerable or endangered while the Saber-Tooth Tiger is long extinct.

▶ Caracal
Native to Africa, the Middle East, Central Asia, and India they are typically nocturnal and highly secretive.
Conservation Status: Least Concern

▶ Cheetah
Native to Africa and central Iran. It is the fastest land animal, capable of running at 80 to 128 km/h (50 to 80 mph),. "cheetah" is derived from Hindustani and means adorned or painted.
Conservation Status: Vulnerable

▶ Clouded Leopard
A medium-sized wild cat occurring from the Himalayan foothills through mainland Southeast Asia into southern China. Considered to form an evolutionary link between the Pantherinae and the Felinae.
Conservation Status: Vulnerable

▶ Cougar
Native to the Americas. Its range spans from the Canadian Yukon to the southern Andes in South America.
Conservation Status: Least Concern

▶ Flat-Headed Cat
Native to the Thai-Malay Peninsula, Borneo, and Sumatra the wild populations is fewer than 2500 individuals due to environment destruction.
Conservation Status: Endangered

▶ Iberian Lynx
Endemic to the Iberian Peninsula in southwestern Europe its population has been threatened because of over-hunting and poaching.
Conservation Status: Endangered

▶ Jaguar
It's range extends from Southwest North America across much of Central America and parts of South America into Argentina. It is the third largest cat species in the world.
Conservation Status: Near Threatened

▶ Kodkod
It's the smallest cat in the Americas and lives primarily in central and southern Chile and marginally in adjoining areas of Argentina.
Conservation Status: Vulnerable

▶ Leopard
Found in a wide range in sub-Saharan Africa, in small parts of Western and Central Asia, on the Indian sub-continent to Southeast and East Asia. Threatened by Habitat loss and illegal poaching.
Conservation Status: Vulnerable

▶ Lion
Lions are found in sub-Saharan Africa and one critically endangered population in western India.
Status: Vulnerable

▶ Oncilla
Ranging from Central America to central Brazil they are listed as vulnerable form habitat lost due to deforestation.
Conservation Status: Vulnerable

▶ Pallas's Cat
A broad, but fragmented Distribution in the grasslands and montane steppes of Central Asia.
Status: Least Concern

▶ Siberian Tiger
Native to the Russian Far East, Northeast China, and possibly North Korea. Only 331–393 adults live in the wild.
Conservation Status: Endangered

▶ Saber-Tooth Tiger
Also called Smilodon it lived in the Americas during the Pleistocene epoch (2.5 mya – 10,000 years ago).
Status: Extinct

▶ Snow Leopard
Native to the mountain ranges of Central and South Asia. Global population is Less than 10,000.
Status: Vulnerable

Wild Cats Index

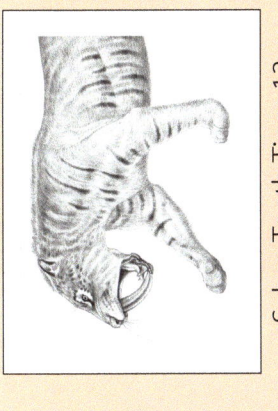
Caracal 1

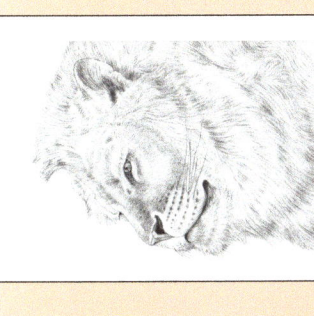
Cheetah 2

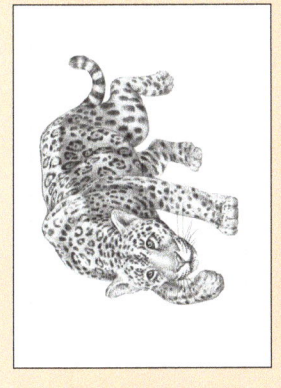
Clouded Leopard 3

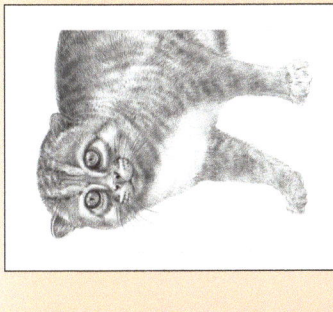
Flat-Headed Cat 4

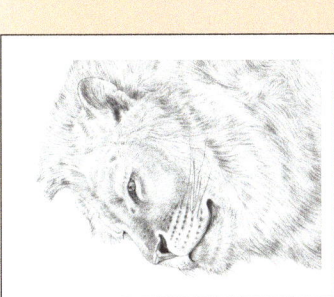
Iberian Lynx 5

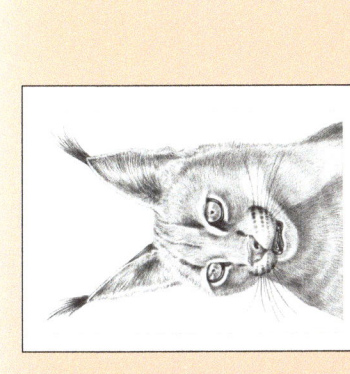
Cougar 6

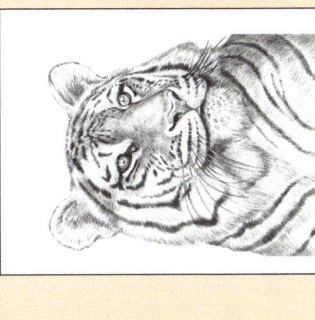
Jaguar 7

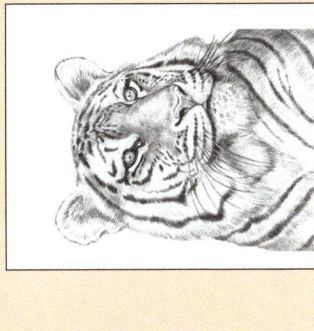
Kodkod 8

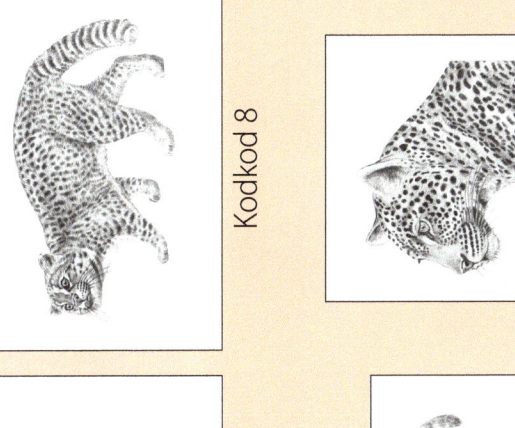
Leopard 9

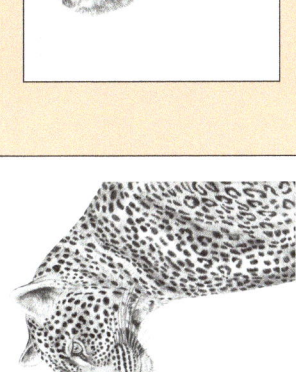
Lion 10

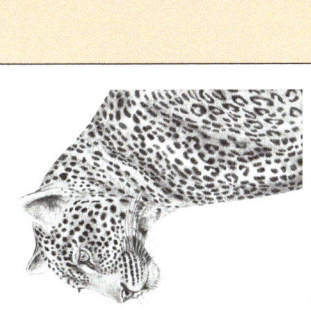
Oncilla 11

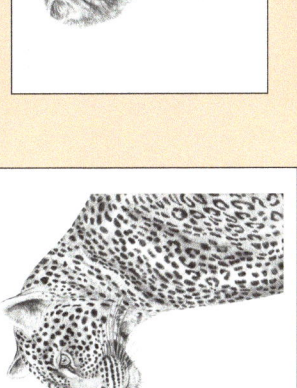
Pallas's Cat 12

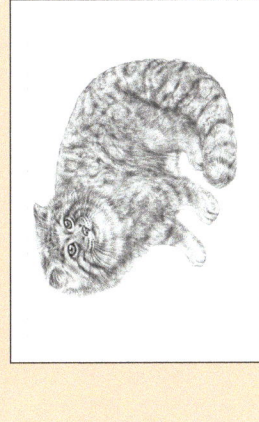
Saber-Tooth Tiger 13

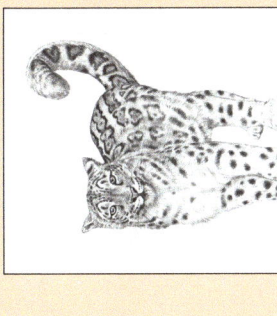
Siberian Tiger 14

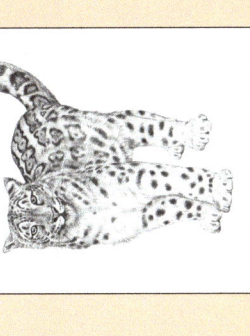
Snow Leopard 15

Caracal

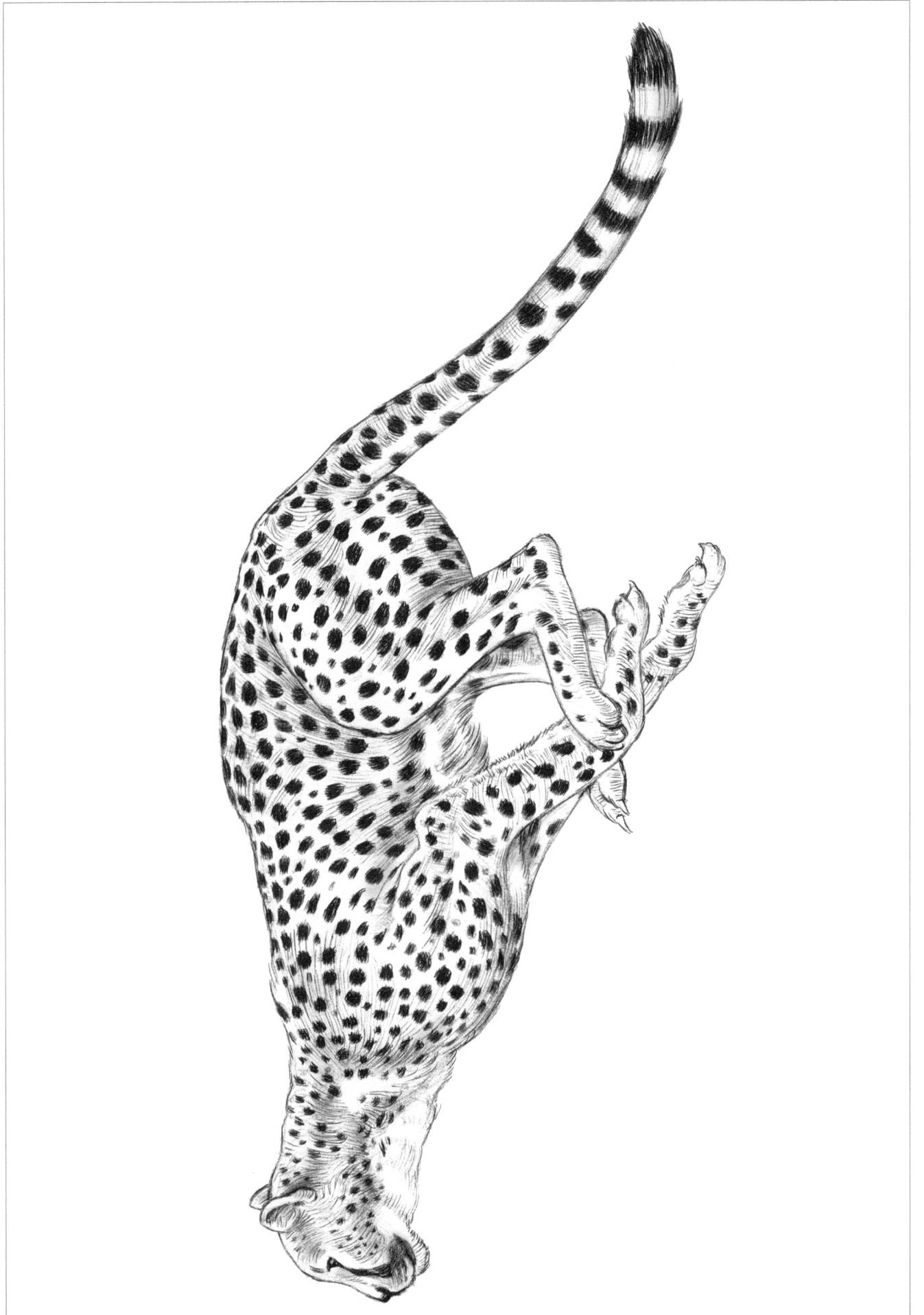

Cheetah

Clouded Leopard

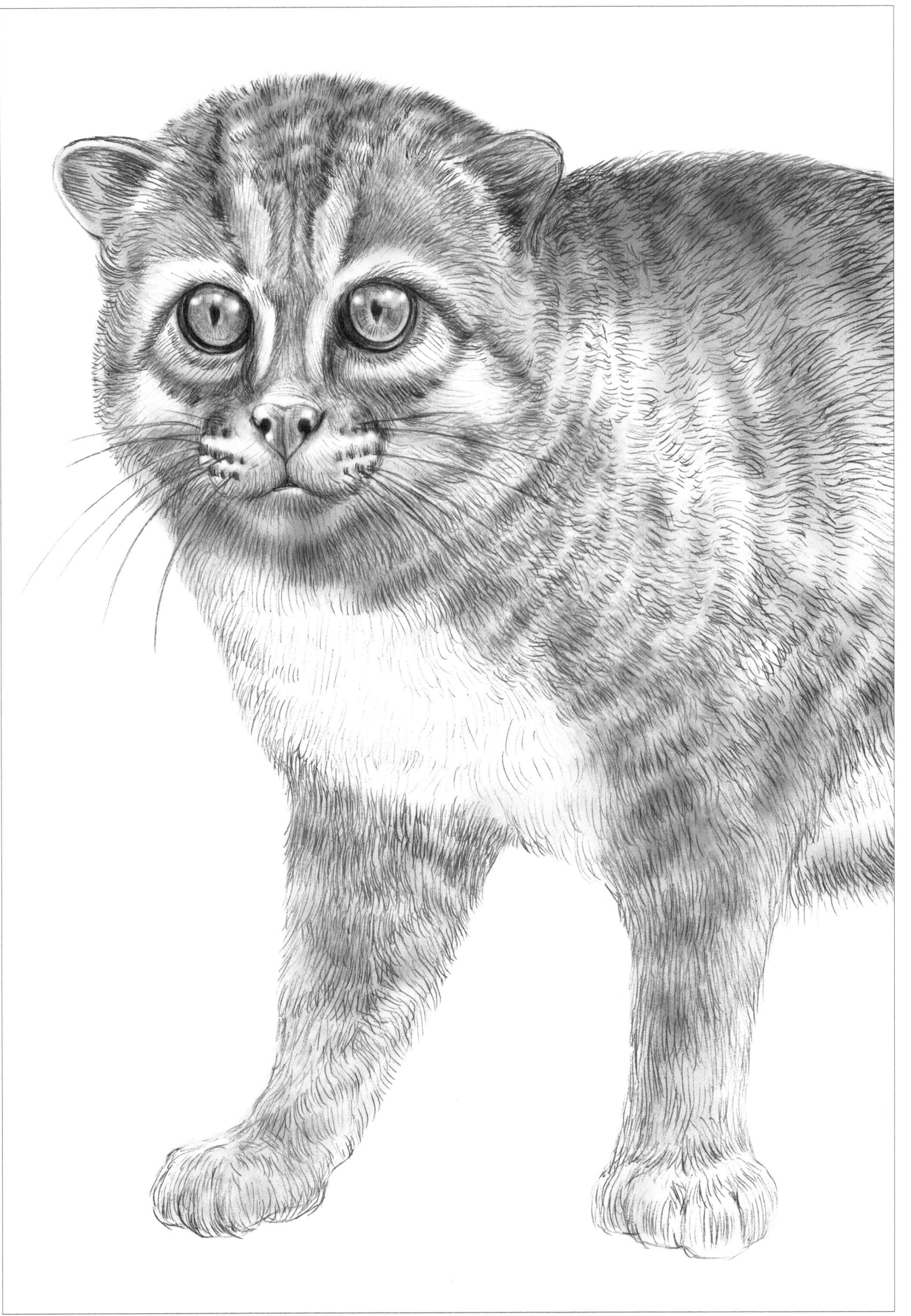

Flat-Headed Cat

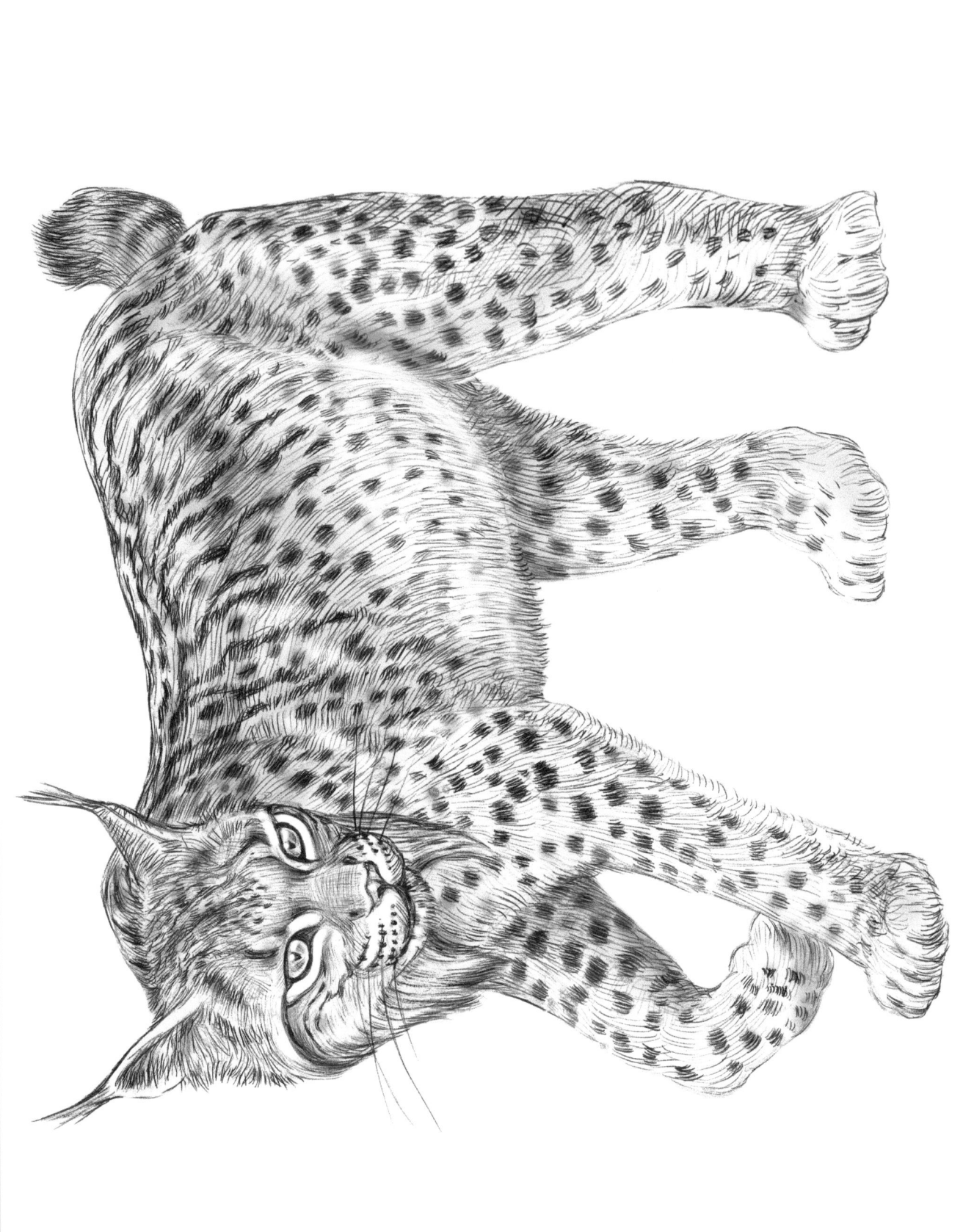

Iberian Lynx

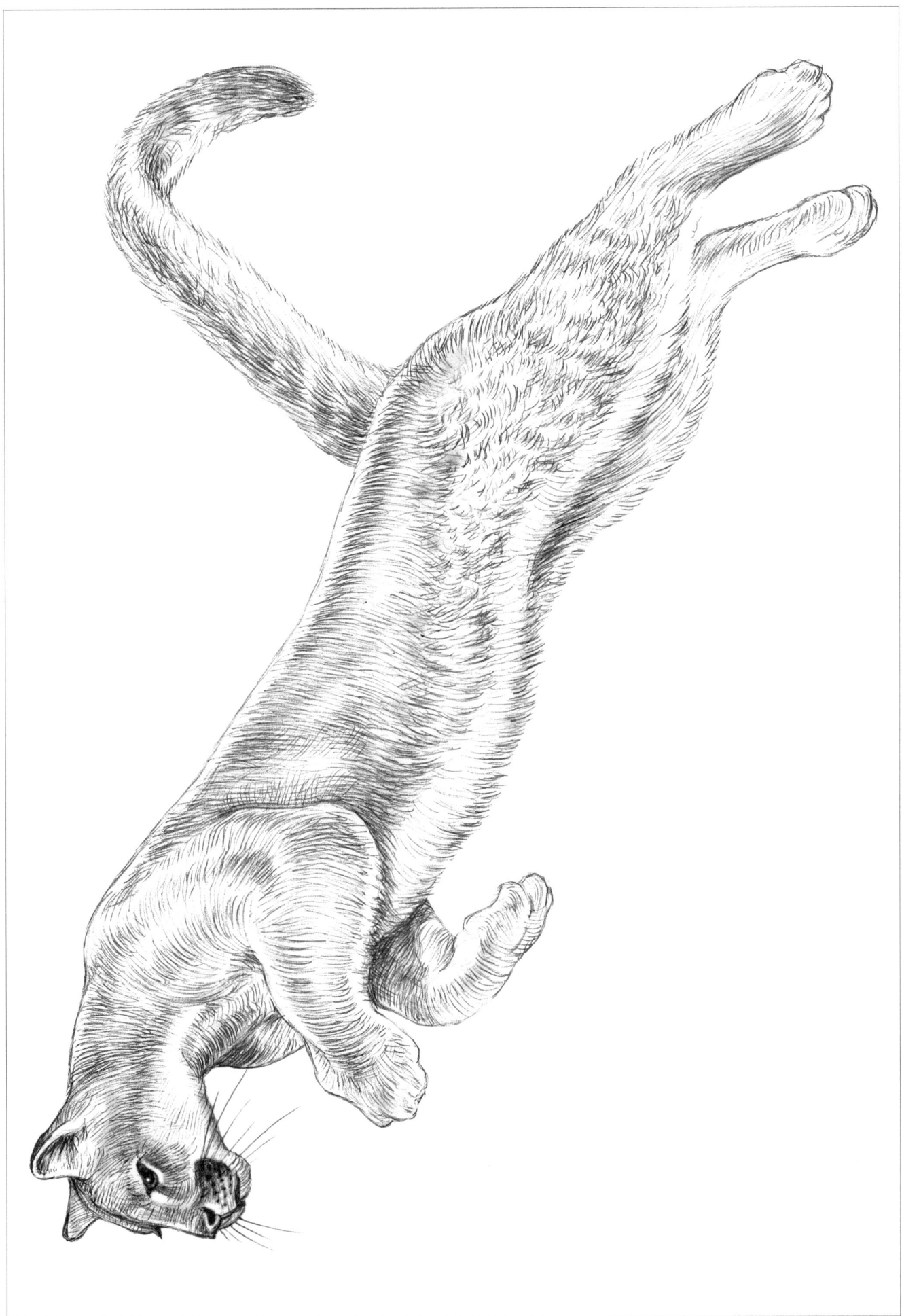

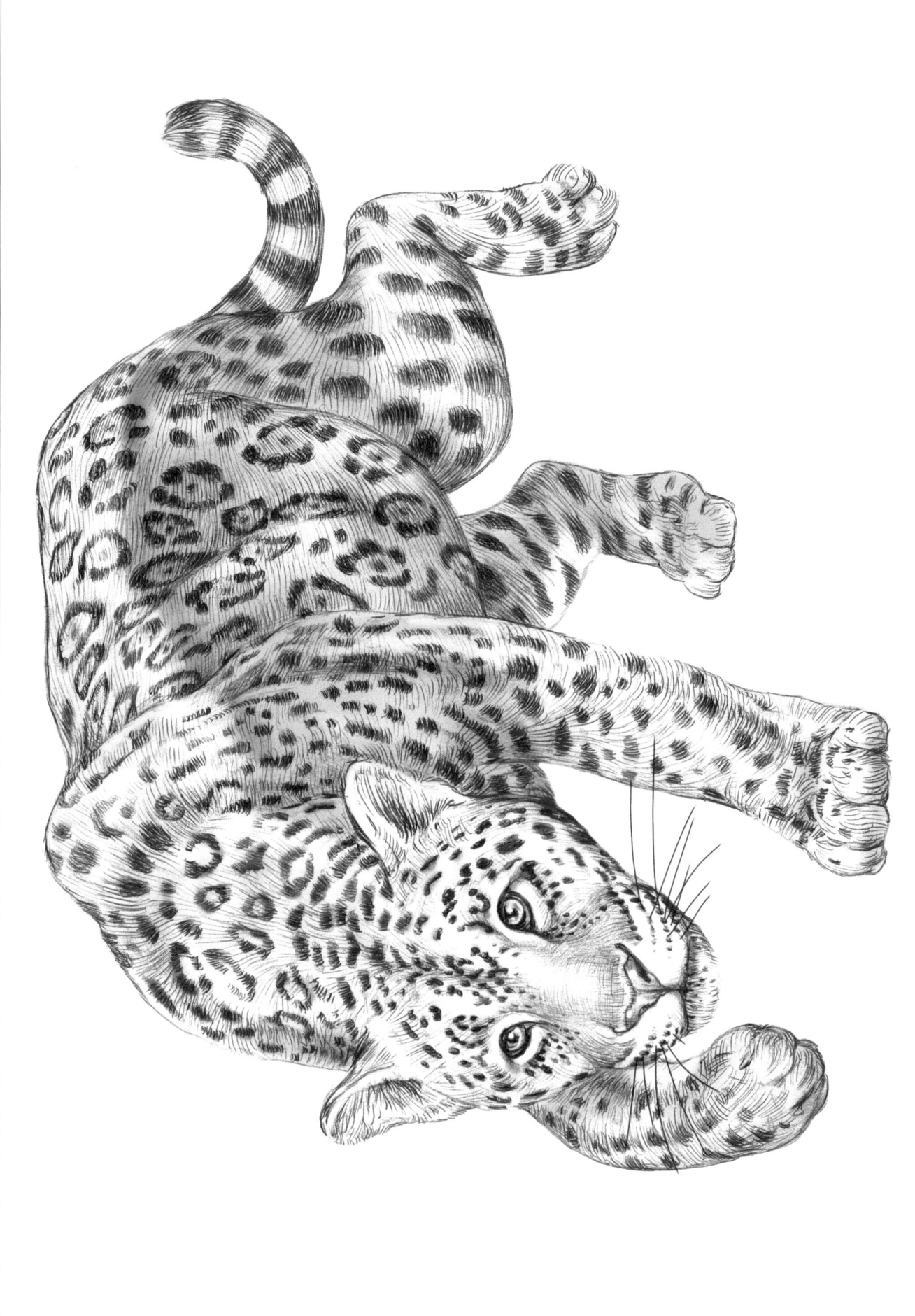

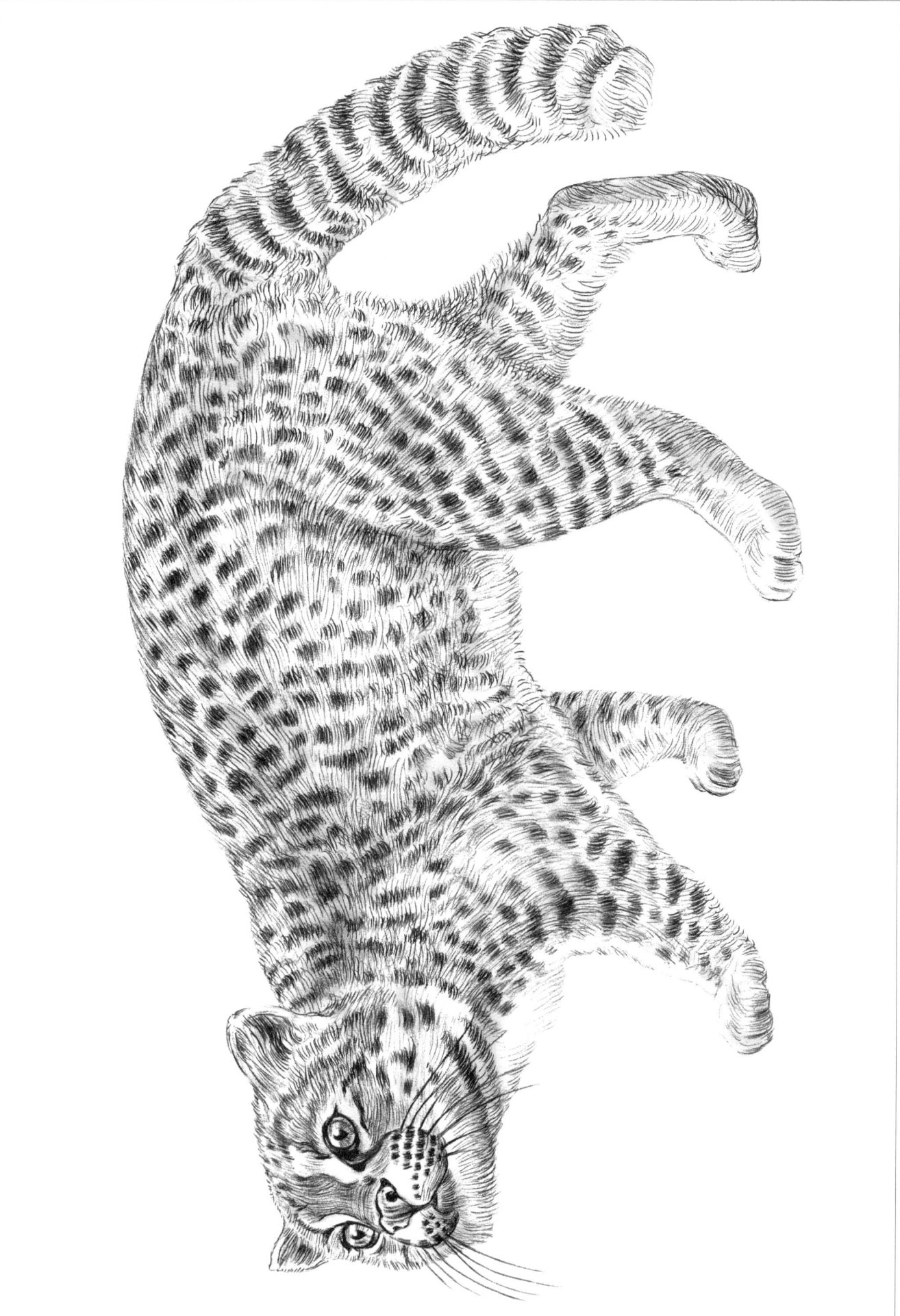

Kodkod

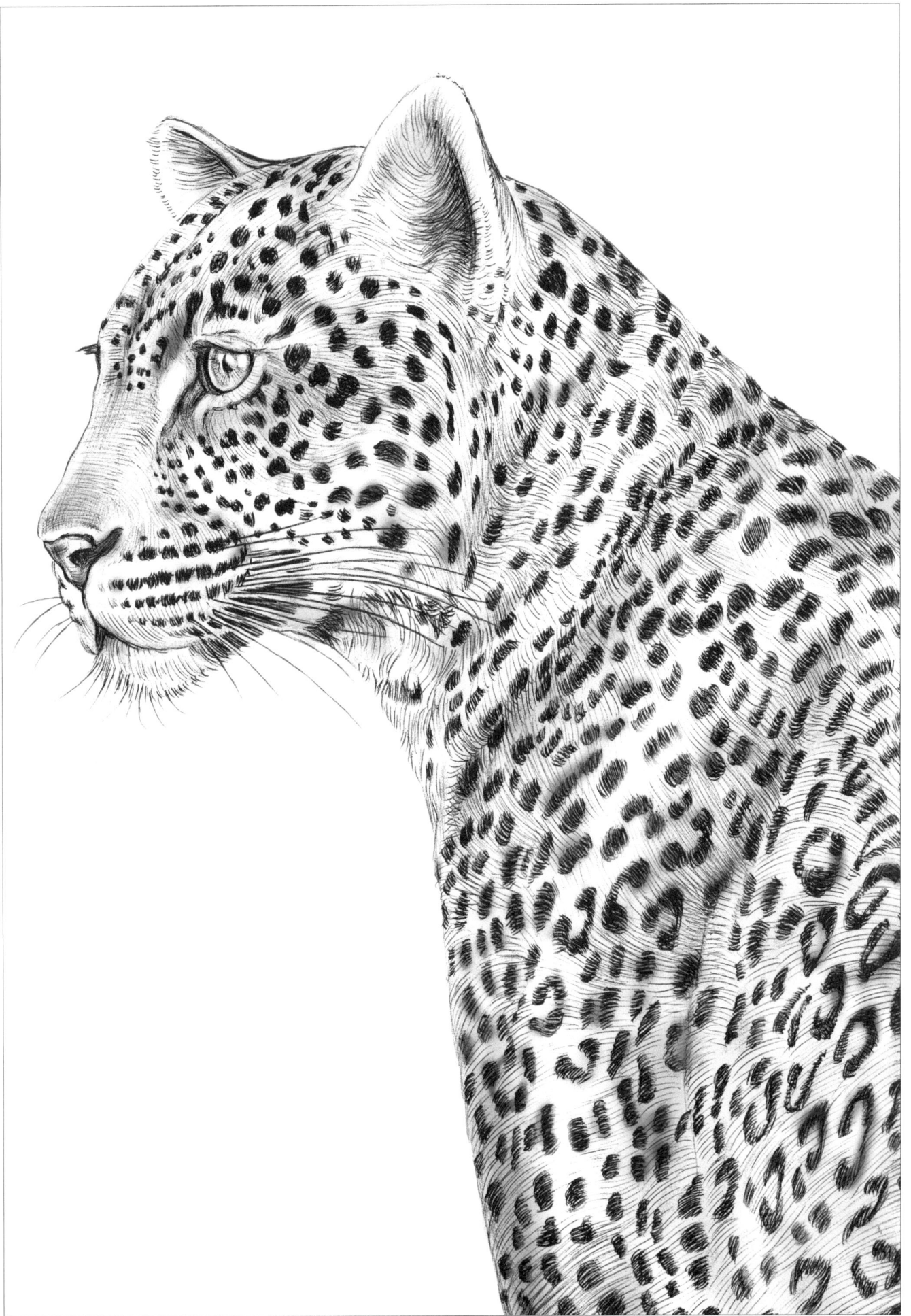

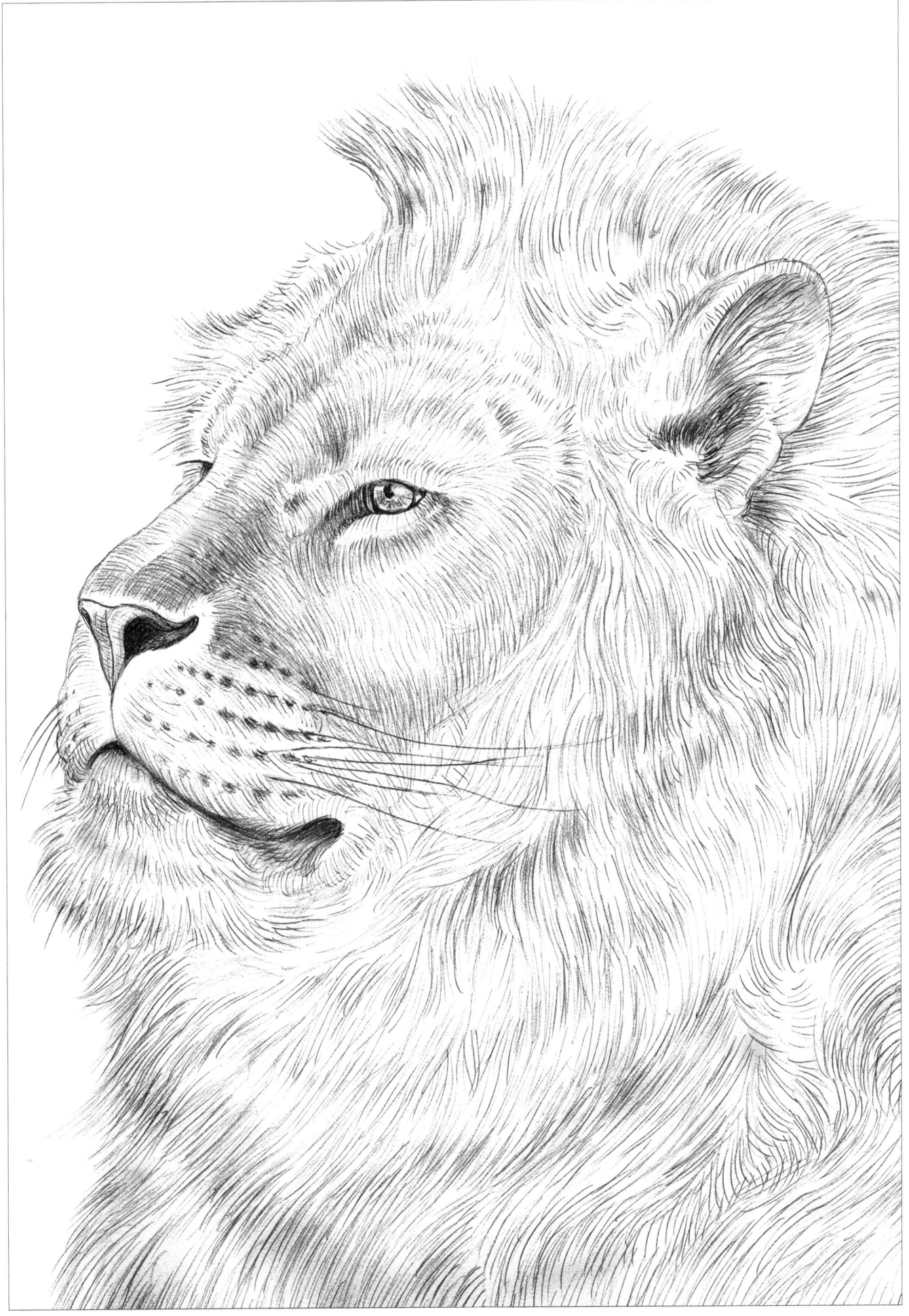

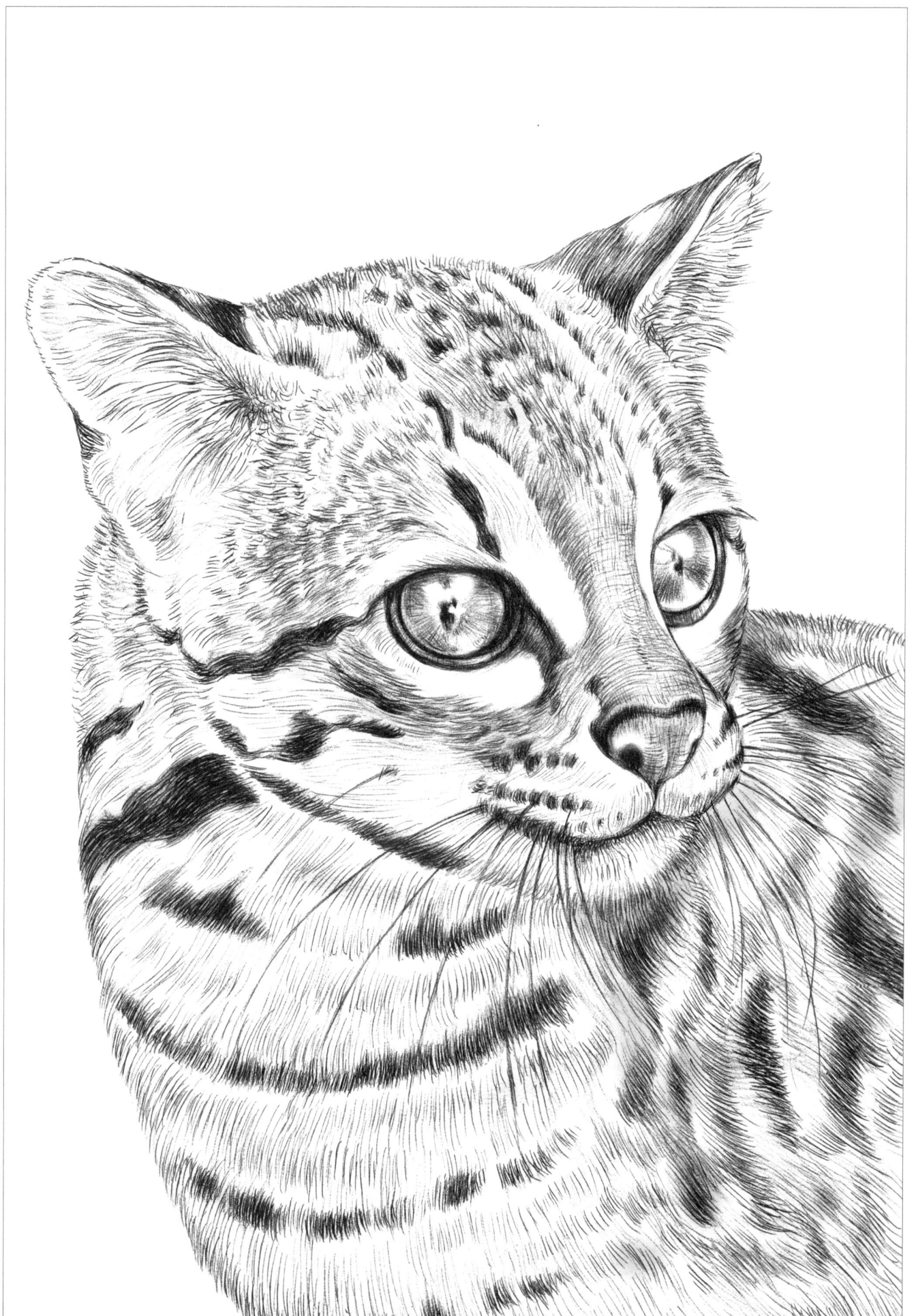

Oncilla

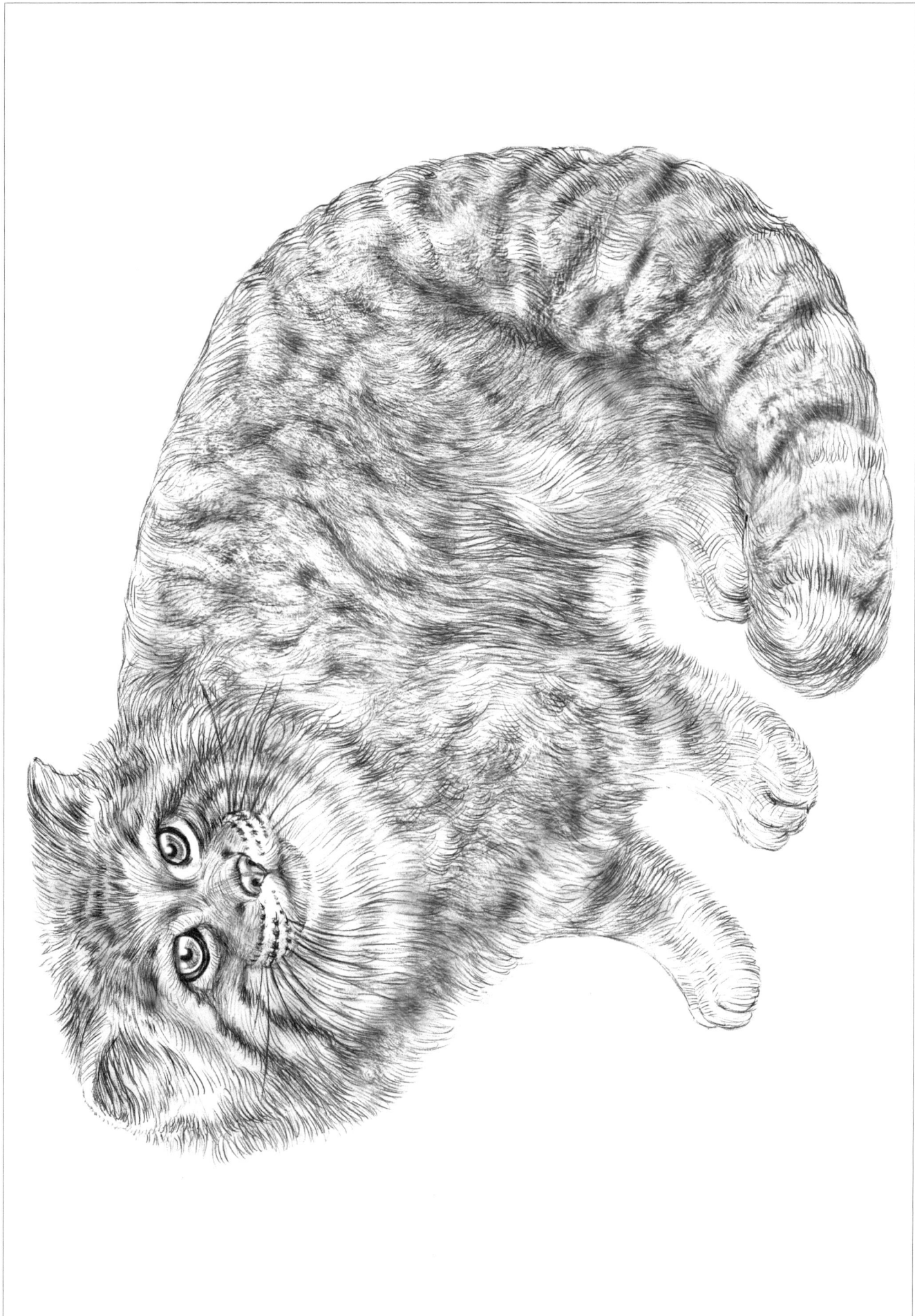

Pallas's Cat

Saber-Tooth Tiger

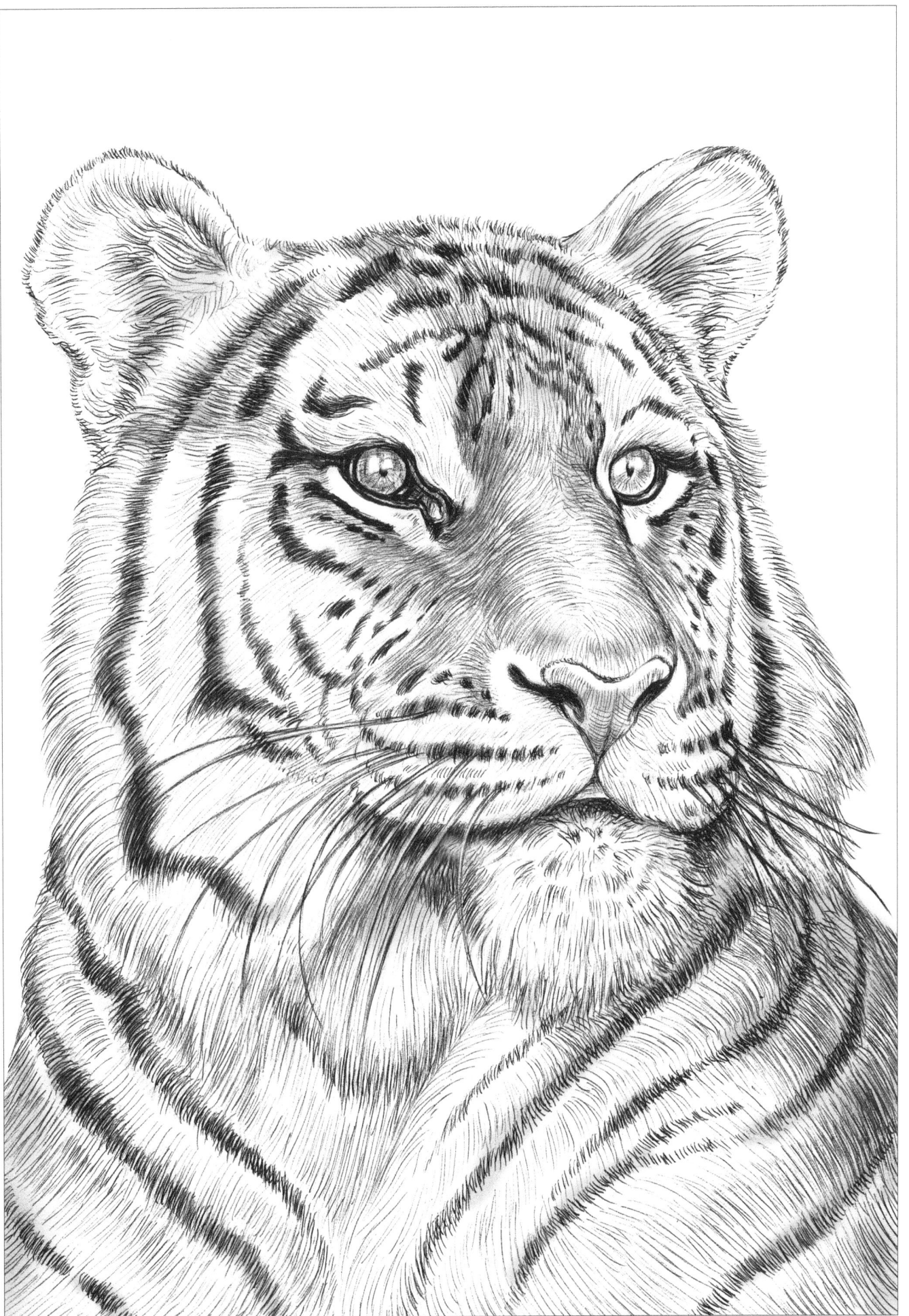

Siberian Tiger

Snow Leopard

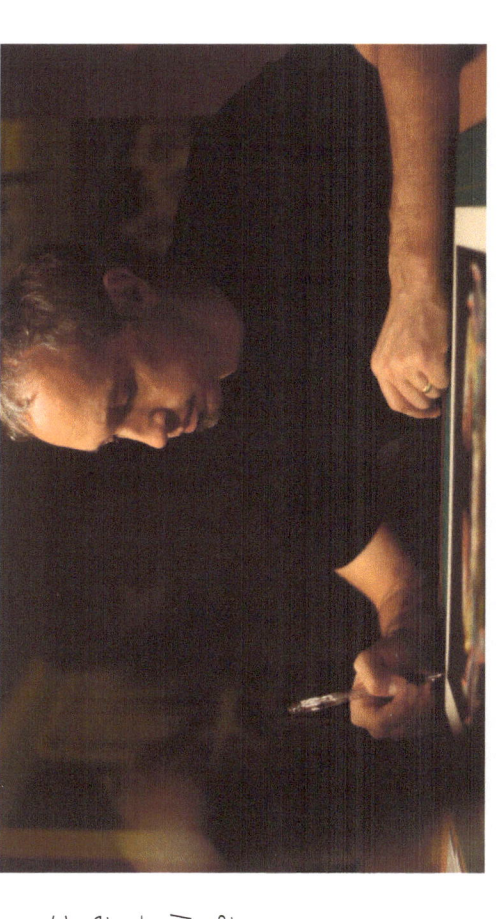

Tim Jeffs is a New York City based artist and illustrator who has been creating dynamic artwork for over 25 years. Animals are a favorite subject matter of his, along with the complex and intricate details these creatures possess. "The incredible diversity and complexity of animals has always intrigued me. They offer endless pleasure to look and marvel upon. In every drawing I try to capture the unique quality of each particular animal. I hope you enjoy my perspective, love and admiration of these incredible creatures."

Visit my website for prints, digital coloring books and coloring lessons:

www.TimJeffsArt.com

Discover the full line of Tim Jeffs' Published Coloring Books

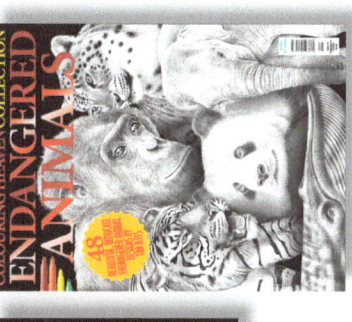
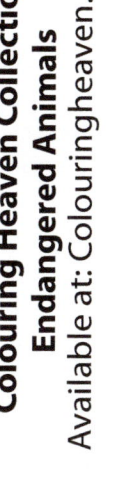

**Colouring Heaven Collection
Endangered Animals**
Available at: Colouringheaven.com

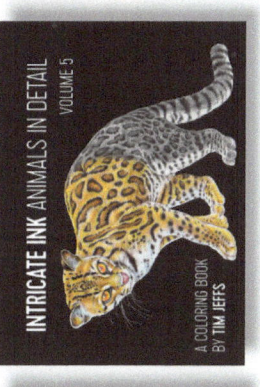
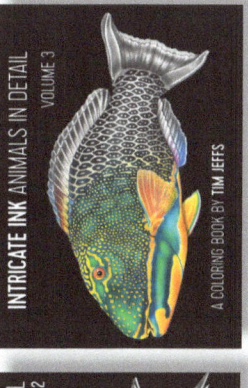
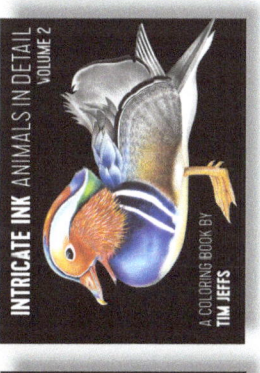
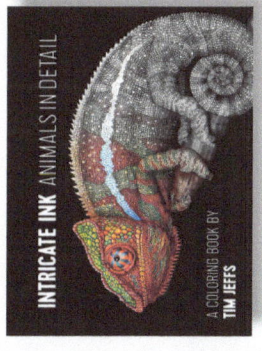

Intricate Ink Animals In Detail Volume 1, 2 3 and 5 Available at:
Pomegranate.com
Amazon.com
Bookdepository.com

Discover Tim Jeffs' Merchandise

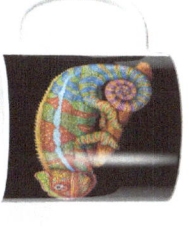

Etsy Shop
www.etsy.com/shop/TimJeffsArt

Society6 Shop
www.society6.com/TimJeffsArt

Redbubble Shop
TimJeffsArt.redbubble.com

Vsual Print Shop
https://vsual.co/shop/tim-jeffs-art

Discover the full line of Tim Jeffs Digital Coloring Books at:
www.TimJeffsArt.com

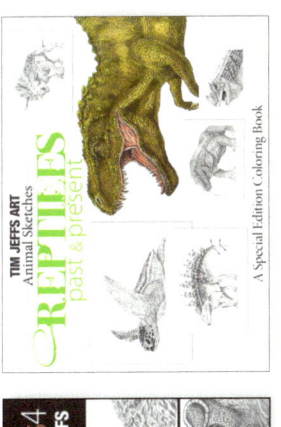
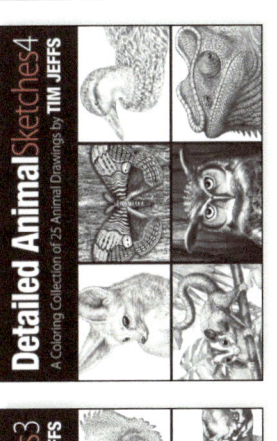
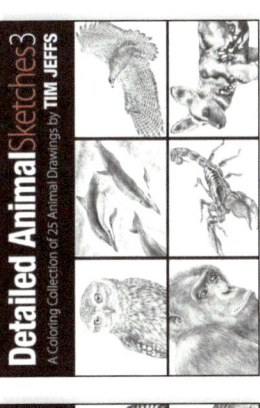
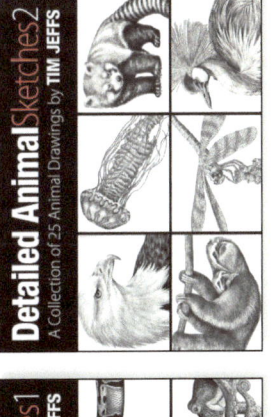
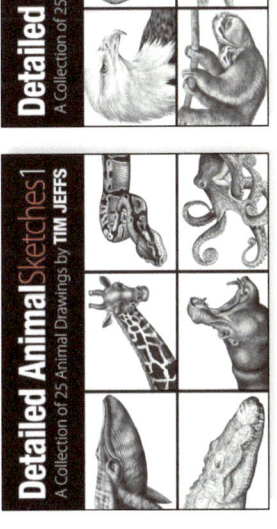

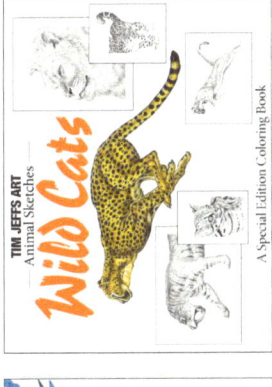
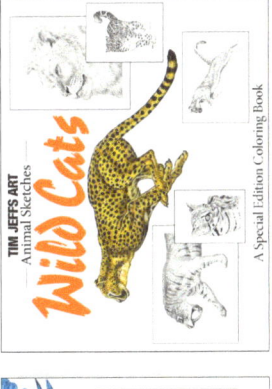
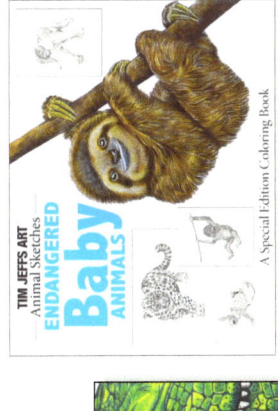
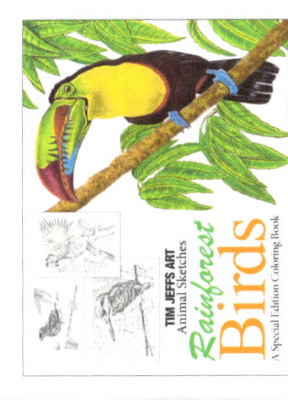

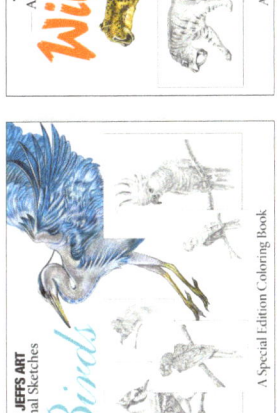
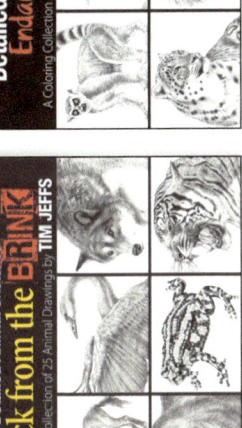

And Coloring Lessons

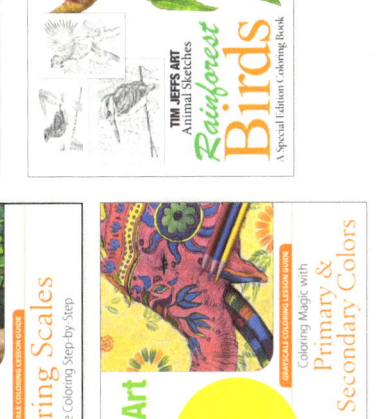
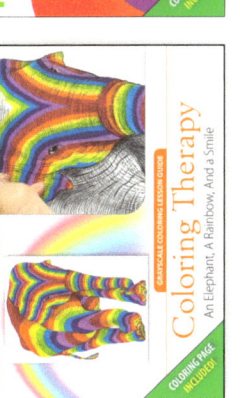

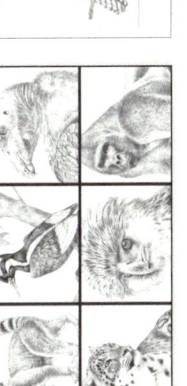
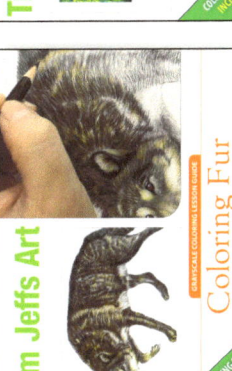

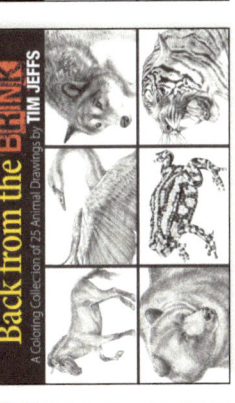
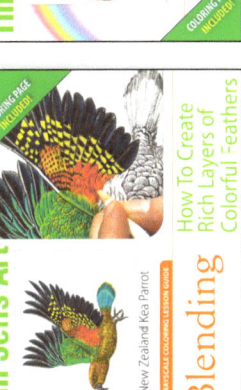

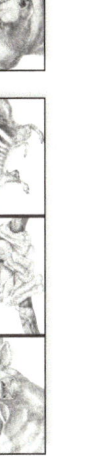
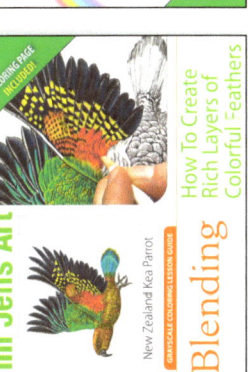

TIM JEFFS ART   Online Resources

Share Your Creativity with the World!

Join the ever-expanding coloring group of animal lovers who inspire each other through their colorings of the animals from Tim's books and lessons. With thousands of members from all around the world, Tim's Facebook group "Intricate Ink Coloring Group" is a creative and safe space where everyone is welcome. Jo Warren, the groups all-inspiring administrator will welcome you in with open arms and is there to encourage everyone to just have fun no matter your coloring skill level. Come join, we can't wait to have you as a member! Join Tim's Facebook Coloring Group at:

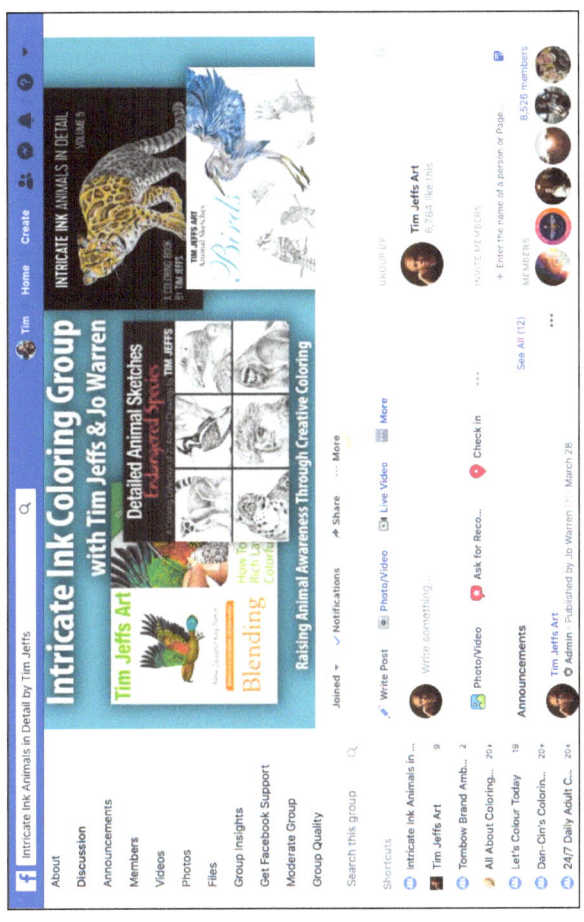

www.facebook.com/groups/intricateink

Visit the Home of Tim Jeffs Art

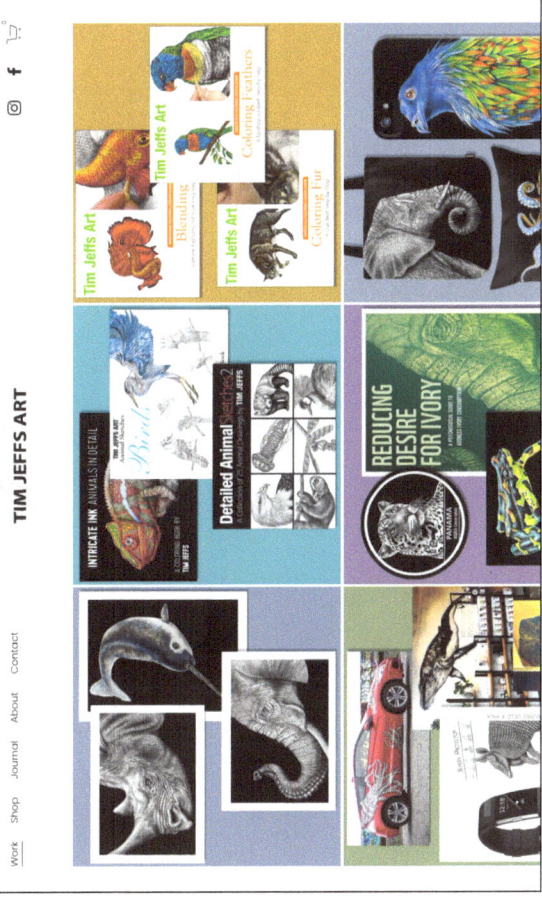

TimJeffsArt.com is my home on the web where I display all of my work and various projects. I hope you can stop by for a visit! You'll find my new shop where signed and unsigned prints of all of my animal drawings are available to purchase, along with the complete library of my digital download coloring books and grayscale coloring lessons. In the conservation section, you can see the projects that I am very proud of. Using my art to preserve wildlife is so important to me.

www.TimJeffsArt.com

www.ingramcontent.com/pod-product-compliance
Lightning Source LLC
Chambersburg PA
CBHW051222220526
45473CB00003B/1132